Harmony of Poetry and Songs

MISS JERRY LEE SCHOCK

Harmony of Poetry and Songs

Copyright © 2022 by Miss Jerry Lee Schock.

Paperback ISBN: 978-1-63812-345-3
Ebook ISBN: 978-1-63812-346-0

All rights reserved. No part in this book may be produced and transmitted in any form or by any means, electronic, or mechanical, including photocopying, recording, or by any information storage and retrieval system, without permission in writing from the copyright owner.

The views expressed in this work are solely those of the author and do not necessarily reflect the views of the publisher hereby disclaims any responsibility for them.

Published by Pen Culture Solutions 06/09/2022

Pen Culture Solutions
1-888-727-7204 (USA)
1-800-950-458 (Australia)
support@penculturesolutions.com

Contents

1. Alex My Blessing 2
2. Another Valley 3
3. Happy Birthday Cindy 6
4. Happy Birthday Bro. Strange 7
5. A Candymaker's Witness 9
6. Celebrate the Saviour 11
7. Chosen 12
8. Comfort Verses from God's Word 18
9. Comfort Verses from God's Word pg.: 2 20
10. God's Answers to the negative things we tell ourselves ... 22
11. Lord, forgive me when I whine 24
12. Happy Birthday My Love 27
13. A Bouquet of Birthday Wishes 28
14. Happy Birthday to my Granddaughter 29
15. The Father Cares 31
16. In loving memory of our precious 33
17. In The Valley 34
18. Bearing the Burden 35
19. The Intercessor 37
20. Jessica 38
21. More Than A Pastor 39
22. As The Eagle Stirreth Her Nest 40
23. Through All Of My Trails 41
24. He's Always Near 42
25. His Love For Me 43
26. I'm Not Alone 44
27. Given to me by the Lord 45
28. Baby In A Manger 46
29. In loving memory of My Precious Sister Nita 47

30. One Heartbeat Away From Heaven 48
31. One Heartbeat Away From Heaven 49
32. Safe and Secure in the Savior 50
33. The Answers 51
34. The Father Cares 52
35. The Gift 53
36. The Gift 54
37. The Greatest Gift Ever Given 55
38. Celebrate the Saviour 56
39. Celebrate the Saviour 57
40. Happy Fathers Day 59
41. Happy Fathers Day 60
42. With Loving Appreciation 61

25 Years of Service

We are at a loss for words- as we honor our Pastor today.
You've spread so much love and happiness all along the way.
Unselfishly your servant heart has taken you over this earth,
There are no words we can say to tell you what you're worth.

Twenty-five years you've given of self,
from a heart of purest gold;
As you've preached, and spread a message
that never will grow old.
You've stayed true to the Word of God
as you sought to do His will-
Unchanging now, for all these years, remaining steady still.

You've walked through many valleys and even shed some tears
Standing only on the Word of God -man you will not fear.
We ask the Lord to bless- as you continue on the way,
With health and multiplied blessings for each and every day.

Galilean Baptist Church
On your 25th anniversary
Jerry L Schock
6/1/08

Alex My Blessing

God sends special people into our lives
to help us along life's way
They're people we can depend on each and every day
I thank God every day as I spend special time in prayer
Asking the Lord to look out for you and meet your every care
My prayer is He protect you and you're walking close to Him
That daily you'll be grateful for the blessings that He sends.
You are one of my special blessings as I led you to the Lord
And I'm trusting He will help you grow
as you daily read His word.
God gave me a special love for you when
he brought you into my life
And I'm grateful for each time you've helped me share the strife
You have borne the burden with me as
you guided me on the way
Make no mistake that love will end only on my dying day.

With all my love and daily prayers as we
continue on our journey toward heaven.
And if I don't see you over here I'll see you over
there. As we await the return of our
precious Lord and Savior Jesus Christ.

> Given to me by the Lord for Alex
> Jerry Lee Schock
> August 26, 2021
> For His glory
> Romans 8:28

Another Valley

My precious Father in heaven I make this petition today,
From the one I love so much please take his pain away.
Give him peace and comfort as You hold him close to You,
If only I could be there that's what I would do.
Let him feel Your presence in a valley that seems so deep
Give him peace and comfort and a very restful sleep.
The only thing in life on which we can depend,
Is the love You promised Your children and that will never end,
Today the clouds have gathered and he cannot see the sun
But brighten up his life Lord as each day is done.
In the valley he is walking You have already gone ahead,
You walked the path before him there is nothing he must dread.
Remind him that every valley has a mountain on each side
Looking ahead with You leading the valley is not so wide.
You promised in the valley you will restore our soul
And our cup will run over with mercy so we can again feel whole.

With love and prayers for Alex as you walk through this
valley with the Lord beside you remember He has promised
He will never leave us or forsake us. PSALM 23

Given to me by the Lord 10/11/21
Jerry :Lee Schock

At this time of year, much focus is on what to buy. The gifts given, will many times outlive their usefulness, later be given away, break, be thrown away, or wear out. So I offer you a "gift" that has no price tag, will not wear out nor outlive its usefulness. I offer you prayer. I want to show you a heart filled with love and concern, especially when you are hurting, and only God knows.

Each time He wakes me in the middle of the night to make intercession –I pray you will remember that He is ever interceding. I pray that in the darkest of nights, when your own faith begins to flicker, God will let you see the candlelight. And you will know He is the light of the world.

I want to pray as you begin an uphill climb, on a road that seems endless, you will find Him as your constant companion. And know He has prepared the way and is there to carry you when it is too hard to walk.

I pray when darkness is closing in around you, He will put stars in your sky to shine brightly. And you will realize He is the star in your world, when all else fails.

I will ask Him that each time you see a sunrise, you will remember it is not only a new day, but a new beginning. And you will let Him bring a new brightness to your day.

I will ask Him to put a song in your heart and on your lips, when others cannot sing. And pray you will let Him be that song.

May the peace and joy of this season
And the Savior, surround you and yours,
In Christian love, Jerry Schock

Happy Birthday Cindy

The words are not so very big
    but the wish is from the heart
As we celebrate your special day –
    I'm glad to have a part.
To simply say you are loved and
    prayed for every day-
And wished the best that life can
    bring-all along the way.

May the Lord hide you safely in the
    shelter of His wings
As you continue on this journey
    enjoying many special things.
May He find new ways to bless you –
    as you make Him your choice;
And may you hear Him whisper
    peace in a still small voice.

Celebrate your life and enjoy what
    He has given you-
For He chose to bless us all
    by sending you –it's true.

Love,
Miss Jerry
2006

Happy Birthday Bro. Strange

So many years you've labored-
As you worked to serve the Lord.
Traveling up and down the road,
You have trusted in His Word.
Sharing the gospel with all you'd meet
Even when Satan tried hard to defeat.
Surely a reward awaits -on the other side-
And special blessings from the Lord,
as in His love you abide.

Your life is a celebration of love
From the Heavenly Father above.
As He daily rewards the effort-
In this life you made to serve.
Someday in Heaven the faces you will see-
Of the ones to whom you witnessed
So in Heaven they could be.

On your 95th Birthday
Bro. Strange because you are loved .
Miss Jerry Schock

March 30, 2006

Broken but repairable I heard the preacher say
The Lord works on His children –as the potter works the clay,
He turns us on that wheel and works with loving hands,
Pulling out the sin, things that keep us from His plan.
When we're on the potter's wheel –the pressure is applied
God molds us into a vessel of honor before

God loves us as a Father and no matter where we have been
He makes us another vessel and loves us through the sin
He does not make us a in a mold as men would have us be
But fashions us for Him –that's best for you and me

He desires us to be close to Him

The potter takes the vessel and forms it into shape –then he dries it lovingly before the fire is applied
Sinners are broken people
As the potters wheel spins he puts pressure on the vessel and molds it and then begins again to mold
God works the same way on us he fashions us a vessel for His glory –another vessel
Sin never leaves us the same –regrets –wish we had –but God
What would I have been had I not gone into sin
Failure need never be final

A Candymaker's Witness

A candy maker in Indiana wanted to make a candy that would be a witness, so he made the Christmas Candy Cane. He incorporated several symbols for the birth, ministry and death of Jesus Christ.

He began with a stick of pure white, hard candy. White to symbolize the Virgin birth and the sinless nature of Jesus; hard to symbolize the Solid Rock, the foundation of the Church, and firmness of the promises of God.

The candy maker made the candy in The Form of the "J" to represent the Precious Name of Jesus, who came to earth as our Saviour. It could also represent the staff of the "Good Shepherd" with which He reaches down into the ditches of the world to lift out the fallen lambs, who like all Sheep have gone astray.

Thinking that the candy was somewhat plain, the candy maker stained it with red stripes. He used three small stripes to show the scourging Jesus received by which we are healed. The large red stripe was for the blood shed by Christ on the Cross so that we could have the promise of eternal life.

Unfortunately, the candy became known as a candy cane – a meaningless decoration seen at Christmas time. But the meaning is still there for those who have "eyes to see and ears to hear". I pray that this symbol will again be used to witness TO THE WONDER OF JESUS AND HIS GREAT LOVE that came down at Christmas and remains the ultimate and dominate force in the universe today

1992 Dicksons

Merry Christmas

Jesus IS the reason
we celebrate

Romans 6:23

Celebrate the Saviour

The world is full of turmoil as it cries out for peace-
But the God of all creation-is in their minds the least.
Many search for things to buy and many overspend-
Finding nothing that will satisy their desire in the end.
*What they really need is **the** gift sent from God above-*
Given for our salvation-sent with lots of love.
There is no price to receive this gift, anyone can pay-
All one needs to do is invite Jesus in today.
He will come into your heart -change your life forever,
And promises a home in Heaven for us to live together.
So focus on the gift of God-to truly satisfy-
*And ask Him into your heart-on Him-you **can** rely.*

May He bless you and yours as we
Celebrate the Saviour
Given to me by the Lord
12/10/11
Jerry L Schock

Chosen

Only GOD can choose the men who will preach the Word.
Now as you follow where He leads, trust only in the Lord.
At times the way you are headed may seem not so clear;
But following Him each day will never lead to fear.
As you're traveling on the road the Lord has set for you,
I'm asking Him "Dear Lord -what am I to do"?
He lets me know that prayer can guide you on the way,
So my promise is to pray for you each and every day.

11/13/2019 For our newly called preachers
Andrew- Billy and -Kevin

I give you this pen -as you use it to be a reminder
of where your trust should be.
***Prov 3:5 Trust in the Lord with all thine heart; and
lean not unto thine own understanding.***

I give you this book so during the times of
disappointment you may be encouraged.
***Psalm 147:3 He healeth the broken in heart,
and bindeth up their wounds.***

I give you a promise of daily prayer to remind you there is always an
intercessor who loves you and is taking your needs to the throne daily.
Gal 6:2 Bear ye one another's burdens, and so fulfil the law of Christ

I give you this money as a small token of my love
for you and in obedience to the Lord.
***1 Peter 1:22 "Having purified your souls by your
obedience to the truth for a sincere brotherly love,
love one another earnestly from a pure heart."***

May He hold you close and strengthen you
daily as you continue to serve Him.
***Rom 12:15 And how shall they preach, except they be sent?
as it is written, How beautiful are the feet of them that preach the
gospel of peace and bring glad tidings of good things!***

7/7/2012

Dear Pastor Rex,

As I prepared for my time with the Lord this morning, I began to look at some of the poetry He has given me through the years. I opened this up which my computer said I worked on last, March 8, 2002, since it was entitled clay. I just wanted to share it since I am still waiting for the Lord to give me the rest of the poem for your sermon. As the little poem came I searched for scriptures on the potter and the clay and copied them all evidently.

I know the Holy Spirit will bless again tomorrow as you come to the pulpit to feed us, surrendered to be used of God, as always. I again pray for spiritual, physical and mental strength for you and Jessica, as I do every day, trusting that God hears and knowing He answers that prayer.

I pray He will just pour the blessings of Heaven over you like a sweet honey flowing and cover you over with His love and peace, as we await His coming and seek to see the lost saved and Christians grow in grace and knowledge.

Remember when satan tries to discourage you there is always someone standing in the gap for you, seeking His face daily for you.

With much love and daily prayer,

For His Glory
Miss Jerry

March 8, 2002

Like me it appears to be just a useless lump of clay-and quite a sticky mess,
Laying around until the hand of the Master –begins to work it –I guess

Jer. 18:4 "And the vessel that he made of clay was marred in the hand of the potter:
so he made it again…" this time in the image of our Heavenly Father
Rom. 9:21: "Hath not the potter power over the clay,…" as He begins shape and mold,
Us into a vessel of honour, that will be beautiful to behold
Is. 64:8 "But now, O Lord, thou art our father; we are the clay and thou our potter;
and we are all the work of they hand." As we wait so still while you work and plan

> One day the Father began to make a special thing for you and me
> He fashioned and He molded it – as carefully as could be
> It would hold a special meaning throughout all eternity,
> As He molded it to perfection –a very beautiful tree

1 Kings 7:46 In the plain of Jordan did the king cast them, in the clay ground between Succoth and Zarthan.
2 Chronicles 4:17 In the plain of Jordan did the king cast them, in the clay ground between Succoth and Zeredathah.
Job 4:19 How much less in them that dwell in houses of clay, whose foundation is in the dust, which are crushed before the moth?
Job 10:9 Remember, I beseech thee, that thou hast made me as the clay; and wilt thou bring me into dust again?
Job 13:12 Your remembrances are like unto ashes, your bodies to bodies of clay.
Job 27:16 Though he heap up silver as the dust, and prepare raiment as the clay;
Job 33:6 Behold, I am according to thy wish in God's stead: I also am formed out of the clay.
Job 38:14 It is turned as clay to the seal; and they stand as a garment.
Psalms 40:2 He brought me up also out of an horrible pit, out of the miry clay, and set my feet upon a rock, and established my goings.

Isaiah 29:16 Surely your turning of things upside down shall be esteemed as the potter's clay: for shall the work say of him that made it, He made me not? or shall the thing framed say of him that framed it, He had no understanding?

Isaiah 41:25 I have raised up one from the north, and he shall come: from the rising of the sun shall he call upon my name: and he shall come upon princes as upon morter, and as the potter treadeth clay.

Isaiah 45:9 Woe unto him that striveth with his Maker! Let the potsherd strive with the potsherds of the earth. Shall the clay say to him that fashioneth it, What makest thou? or thy work, He hath no hands?

Isaiah 64:8 But now, O LORD, thou art our father; we are the clay, and thou our potter; and we all are the work of thy hand.

Jeremiah 18:4 And the vessel that he made of clay was marred in the hand of the potter: so he made it again another vessel, as seemed good to the potter to make it.

Jeremiah 18:6 O house of Israel, cannot I do with you as this potter? saith the LORD. Behold, as the clay is in the potter's hand, so are ye in mine hand, O house of Israel.

Jeremiah 43:9 Take great stones in thine hand, and hide them in the clay in the brickkiln, which is at the entry of Pharaoh's house in Tahpanhes, in the sight of the men of Judah;

Daniel 2:33 His legs of iron, his feet part of iron and part of clay.

Daniel 2:34 Thou sawest till that a stone was cut out without hands, which smote the image upon his feet that were of iron and clay, and brake them to pieces.

Daniel 2:35 Then was the iron, the clay, the brass, the silver, and the gold, broken to pieces together, and became like the chaff of the summer threshingfloors; and the wind carried them away, that no place was found for them: and the stone that smote the image became a great mountain, and filled the whole earth.

Daniel 2:41 And whereas thou sawest the feet and toes, part of potters' clay, and part of iron, the kingdom shall be divided; but there shall be in it of the strength of the iron, forasmuch as thou sawest the iron mixed with miry clay.

Daniel 2:42 And as the toes of the feet were part of iron, and part of clay, so the kingdom shall be partly strong, and partly broken.

Daniel 2:43 And whereas thou sawest iron mixed with miry clay, they shall mingle themselves with the seed of men: but they shall not cleave one to another, even as iron is not mixed with clay.

Daniel 2:45 Forasmuch as thou sawest that the stone was cut out of the mountain without hands, and that it brake in pieces the iron, the brass, the clay, the silver, and the gold; the great God hath made known to the king what shall come to pass hereafter: and the dream is certain, and the interpretation thereof sure.

Nahum 3:14 Draw thee waters for the siege, fortify thy strong holds: go into clay, and tread the morter, make strong the brickkiln.

Habakkuk 2:6 Shall not all these take up a parable against him, and a taunting proverb against him, and say, Woe to him that increaseth that which is not his! how long? and to him that ladeth himself with thick clay!

John 9:6 When he had thus spoken, he spat on the ground, and made clay of the spittle, and he anointed the eyes of the blind man with the clay,

John 9:11 He answered and said, A man that is called Jesus made clay, and anointed mine eyes, and said unto me, Go to the pool of Siloam, and wash: and I went and washed, and I received sight.

John 9:14 And it was the sabbath day when Jesus made the clay, and opened his eyes.

John 9:15 Then again the Pharisees also asked him how he had received his sight. He said unto them, He put clay upon mine eyes, and I washed, and do see.

Psalms 2:9 Thou shalt break them with a rod of iron; thou shalt dash them in pieces like a potter's vessel.

Isaiah 29:16 Surely your turning of things upside down shall be esteemed as the potter's clay: for shall the work say of him that made it, He made me not? or shall the thing framed say of him that framed it, He had no understanding?

Isaiah 41:25 I have raised up one from the north, and he shall come: from the rising of the sun shall he call upon my name: and he shall come upon princes as upon morter, and as the potter treadeth clay.

Isaiah 64:8 But now, O LORD, thou art our father; we are the clay, and thou our potter; and we all are the work of thy hand.

Jeremiah 18:2 Arise, and go down to the potter's house, and there I will cause thee to hear my words.

Jeremiah 18:3 Then I went down to the potter's house, and, behold, he wrought a work on the wheels.

Jeremiah 18:4 And the vessel that he made of clay was marred in the hand of the potter: so he made it again another vessel, as seemed good to the potter to make it.

Jeremiah 18:6 O house of Israel, cannot I do with you as this potter? saith the LORD. Behold, as the clay is in the potter's hand, so are ye in mine hand, O house of Israel.

Jeremiah 19:1 Thus saith the LORD, Go and get a potter's earthen bottle, and take of the ancients of the people, and of the ancients of the priests;

Jeremiah 19:11 And shalt say unto them, Thus saith the LORD of hosts; Even so will I break this people and this city, as one breaketh a potter's vessel, that cannot be made whole again: and they shall bury them in Tophet, till there be no place to bury.

Lamentations 4:2 The precious sons of Zion, comparable to fine gold, how are they esteemed as earthen pitchers, the work of the hands of the potter!

Zechariah 11:13 And the LORD said unto me, Cast it unto the potter: a goodly price that I was prised at of them. And I took the thirty pieces of silver, and cast them to the potter in the house of the LORD.

Matthew 27:7 And they took counsel, and bought with them the potter's field, to bury strangers in.

Matthew 27:10 And gave them for the potter's field, as the Lord appointed me.

Romans 9:21 Hath not the potter power over the clay, of the same lump to make one vessel unto honour, and another unto dishonour?

Revelation 2:27 And he shall rule them with a rod of iron; as the vessels of a potter shall they be broken to shivers: even as I received of my Father.

Comfort Verses from God's Word

Psalms 32:7 Thou art my hiding place; thou shalt preserve me from trouble; thou shalt compass me about with songs of deliverance. Selah.
Psalms 34:4 I sought the LORD, and he heard me, and delivered me from all my fears.
Psalms 15 And call upon me in the day of trouble: I will deliver thee, and thou shalt glorify me.
Psalms 57:1 Be merciful unto me, O God, be merciful unto me: for my soul trusteth in thee: yea, in the shadow of thy wings will I make my refuge, until these calamities be overpast.
Psalms 63:7 Because thou hast been my help, therefore in the shadow of thy wings will I rejoice.
Psalms 71:21 Thou shalt increase my greatness, and comfort me on every side.
Psalm 91

1 He that dwelleth in the secret place of the most High shall abide under the shadow of the Almighty.
2 I will say of the LORD, He is my refuge and my fortress: my God; in him will I trust.
3 Surely he shall deliver thee from the snare of the fowler, and from the noisome pestilence.
4 He shall cover thee with his feathers, and under his wings shalt thou trust: his truth shall be thy shield and buckler.
5 Thou shalt not be afraid for the terror by night; nor for the arrow that flieth by day;
6 Nor for the pestilence that walketh in darkness; nor for the destruction that wasteth at noonday.
9 Because thou hast made the LORD, which is my refuge, even the most High, thy habitation;
11 For he shall give his angels charge over thee, to keep thee in all thy ways.
12 They shall bear thee up in their hands, lest thou dash thy foot against a stone.
14 Because he hath set his love upon me, therefore will I deliver him: I will set him on high, because he hath known my name.

15 He shall call upon me, and I will answer him: I will be with him in trouble; I will deliver him, and honour him.

Psalms 119:50 This is my comfort in my affliction: for thy word hath quickened me.
Psalms 119:76 Let, I pray thee, thy merciful kindness be for my comfort, according to thy word unto thy servant.
Psalms 121:1 I will lift up mine eyes unto the hills, from whence cometh my help

4 Behold, he that keepeth Israel shall neither slumber nor sleep.
8 The LORD shall preserve thy going out and thy coming in from this time forth, and even for evermore.

Psalms 139:2 Thou knowest my downsitting and mine uprising, thou understandest my thought afar off.
3 Thou compassest my path and my lying down, and art acquainted with all my ways.
4 For there is not a word in my tongue, but, lo, O LORD, thou knowest it altogether.
5 Thou hast beset me behind and before, and laid thine hand upon me.

Psalms 139:6 Such knowledge is too wonderful for me; it is high, I cannot attain unto it.

7 Whither shall I go from thy spirit? or whither shall I flee from thy presence?
8 If I ascend up into heaven, thou art there: if I make my bed in hell, behold, thou art there.
9 If I take the wings of the morning, and dwell in the uttermost parts of the sea;
10 Even there shall thy hand lead me, and thy right hand shall hold me.
11 If I say, Surely the darkness shall cover me; even the night shall be light about me.

Comfort Verses from God's Word pg.: 2

Isaiah 26:3 Thou wilt keep him in perfect peace, whose mind is stayed on thee: because he trusteth in thee.

Isaiah 40:31 But they that wait upon the LORD shall renew their strength; they shall mount up with wings as eagles; they shall run, and not be weary; and they shall walk, and not faint.

Isaiah 41:18 I will open rivers in high places, and fountains in the midst of the valleys: I will make the wilderness a pool of water, and the dry land springs of water.

Isaiah 43:2 When thou passest through the waters, I will be with thee; and through the rivers, they shall not overflow thee: when thou walkest through the fire, thou shalt not be burned; neither shall the flame kindle upon thee.

Isaiah 49:2 And he hath made my mouth like a sharp sword; in the shadow of his hand hath he hid me, and made me a polished shaft; in his quiver hath he hid me;

Isaiah 51:16 And I have put my words in thy mouth, and I have covered thee in the shadow of mine hand, that I may plant the heavens, and lay the foundations of the earth, and say unto Zion, Thou art my people.

Hebrews 13:5 Let your conversation be without covetousness; and be content with such things as ye have: for he hath said, I will never leave thee, nor forsake thee.

October 5, 2013

As I met with the Lord this morning –after reading Is. 55 –the love and protection of our Lord and Savior and our Father-became so real. He stirred my heart and I wrote to Him as I prayed, then I thought-some of my brothers and sisters may be able to use what The Lord gave me-even though it is not a poem –as I usually share-it is from the heart and my prayer is it will help someone who may be struggling.

ALWAYS remember that the Lord is near-He always watches and He will not let you fall without catching you in loving arms –and as you walk through whatever valley He is allowing –remember He walked ahead of you and He will NEVER allow anything to come your way that HE cannot handle. Thank God there are no limits for Him.

Thank You Lord, for always being there. Even when I cannot see the way –You always doeven when I have lost sight of what it Can be –You have not-even when I am hurting-You begin the healing-even when I am afraid-You calm the fear-even when I am not sure of Why things happen when they do –many times You later show me the Why and it is always a reminder of Romans 8:28. Whether in sorrow-in pain-in uncertainty-no matter what the situation-the time or the circumstances-You ALWAYS! do the right thing for me, even when I cannot –You CAN and Will and Do.

Help me to NEVER miss that special touch You send my way when I see the beauty You have created around me. Even that beauty CANNOT be without You. Lord please help me to NEVER lose sight of Calvary and what You have done for me, to NEVER let a day pass without that sweet Holy Spirit leading me to do for others-in prayer-in word and in deed. Help me to never walk too far from Calvary and to ALWAYS remember WHOSE I am.

Just Your daughter,
Jerry

God's Answers to the negative things we tell ourselves

"It's impossible"
All things are possible (Luke 18:27)

"I'm too tired"
I will give you rest (Matthew 11:28-30)

"Nobody really loves me"
I love you (John 3:16 & John 13:34)

"I can't go on"
My grace is sufficient (II Corinthians 12:9 & Psalm 91:15)

"I can't figure things out"
I will direct your steps (Proverbs 3:5-6)

"I can't do it"
You can do all things (Phillipians 4:13)

"I'm not able"
I am able (II Corinthians 9:8)

"It's not worth it"
It will be worth it (Romans 8:28)

"I can't forgive myself"
I forgive you (I John 1:9 & Romans 8:1)

"I can't manage"
I will supply all your needs (Phillipians 4:19)

"I'm afraid"
I have not given you a spirit of fear (II Timothy 1:7)

"I'm always worried and frustrated"
Cast all your cares on Me (I Peter 5:7)

"I don't have enough faith"
I've given everyone a measure of faith (Romans 12:3)

"I'm not smart enough"
I give you wisdom (I Corinthians 1:30)

"I feel all alone"
I will never leave you or forsake you (Hebrews 13:5)

Lord, forgive me when I whine

Today, upon a bus, I saw a girl with golden hair.
I envied her, she seemed so gay,
and wished I was as fair.
When suddenly she rose to leave,
I saw her hobble down the aisle.
She had one leg and wore a crutch.
But as she passed, a smile.

Oh, God, forgive me when I whine.
I have 2 legs, the world is mine.

I stopped to buy some candy.
The lad who sold it had such charm.
I talked with him, he seemed so glad.
If I were late, it'd do no harm.
And as I left, he said to me,
"I thank you, you've been so kind.
It's nice to talk with folks like you.
You see," he said, "I'm blind."

Oh, God, forgive me when I whine.
I have 2 eyes, the world is mine.

Later while walking down the street,
I saw a child with eyes of blue.
He stood and watched the others play.
He did not know what to do.
I stopped a moment and then I said,
"Why don't you join the others, dear?"
He looked ahead without a word.
And then I knew, he couldn't hear.

Oh, God, forgive me when I whine.
I have 2 ears, the world is mine.
With feet to take me where I'd go.
With eyes to see the sunset's glow.
With ears to hear what I'd know.
Oh, God, forgive me when I whine.
I've been blessed indeed, the world is mine.

25 Years of Service

We are at a loss for words- as we honor our Pastor today.
You've spread so much love and happiness all along the way.
Unselfishly your servant heart has taken you over this earth,
There are no words we can say to tell you what you're worth.

Twenty-five years you've given of self, from a heart of purest gold;
As you've preached, and spread a message that never will grow old.
You've stayed true to the Word of God as you sought to do His will-
Unchanging now, for all these years, remaining steady still.

You've walked through many valleys and even shed some tears
Standing only on the Word of God -man you will not fear.
We ask the Lord to bless- as you continue on the way,
With health and multiplied blessings for each and every day.

THANK YOU FOR GIVING TO THE LORD

Galilean Baptist Church
On your 25th anniversary
Tolbert Moore
Jerry L Schock
6/1/08

Happy Birthday My Love

To just say happy birthday seems not enough to do
Sending birthday wishes to the one I love so true.
So I'll just say happy birthday to my one and only love.
Knowing you were heaven sent from the Lord above.
You've made my life complete and I've given you my heart-
Praying we're together forever -nevermore to part.
Until God put you in my life giving me a love so real
Never dreaming ever it was something I would feel.
Life just seems so empty when your voice I cannot hear
Yet just one word from you draws us oh so near
So happy birthday sweetheart to the man I love
As I daily thank the Lord for you in heaven above.

Happy birthday Alex I pray we have
many more together forever.
With all my love and devotion,
Jerry Lee

A Bouquet of Birthday Wishes

For our special sister Lessie

Today as you turn 70--the years have gone oh so fast,
But we have such good memories of things now in the past.
You faithfully served the Lord raising your children alone,
Then saw the blessings of the Lord as they had children of their own.
Each time one of us had a need -you were always there-
Staying right beside us and always faithful in prayer.
We've been through so very many things -even heartache and pain.
But watched as the Father healed you-and made you whole again.
In time God gave you a home-so beautiful to behold.
We've shared such good times there-too many to be told.
Today these wishes from the heart-come with all our love
We ask the Father for many more years and blessings from above.

Happy Birthday Lessie
From all your sisters
Ollie -Linda-Jane-Jerry
Is 40:31

Happy Birthday to my Granddaughter

God made a special girl one day just for me
Running to and fro doing for others you see,
And put a love deep in her heart unlike any other-
Nana is what I am to her-as much as any grandmother.
Daring to be different as she serves our precious Lord
Daring to depend -only on His Word.
And always she is striving to serve Him in every way
Under every circumstance-
Giving every day.
He truly blessed my life the day He brought her in.
The love is oh so strong for me,
Even in times of stress
Really this special girl is nothing but the Best.
I Love you Gladys, more than you will ever know.

Your Nana
06/22/2019

HOW TO ACCEPT JESUS

For God so loved the world, that he gave his only begotten Son, that whosoeverbelieveth in Him should not perish, but have everlasting life.
John 3:16

If you confess with your mouth that Jesus is Lord, and believe in your heart that God has raised Him from the dead,you will be saved."
Romans 10:9

PRAY THIS PRAYER:

Dear Jesus, I am a sinner. I believe that You died and rose from the dead to save me from my sins. I want to be with you in heaven forever. Jesus forgive me of all my sins that I have committed against You.I open my heart to You now and ask You to come into my heart as my personal Lord and Savior.
In Jesus name, Amen

The Father Cares

I do not know what trial you face or the road that you must take
But I know the Father in Heaven –cannot make a mistake.
No trials can come our way –or touch us in this place
Except it first is approved above-at the Throne of Grace.
So when the road is hard to walk and the pain you cannot bear-
Know the Father in Heaven –He cares and is always there.
He walked the road before you and knows each step ahead-
Just hold on my precious loved one-there is nothing you should dread.
Hold that precious promise in your heart that you'll never be alone-
And take the burdens to the Lord-lay them at the throne.

Given to me by the Lord
Jerry Lee Schock
02/15/21

I see the countless Christmas Trees around the world below,
with tiny lights, like heaven's stars, reflecting on the snow.

The sight is so spectacular, please wipe away that tear,
for I am spending Christmas with Jesus Christ this year.

I hear the many Christmas songs that people hold so dear,
but the sounds of music can't compare with the Christmas choir up here.

I have no words to tell you, the joy their voices bring,
for it is beyond description, to hear the angels sing.

I know how much you miss me. I see the pain inside your heart,
but I am not so far away. We really aren't apart.

So be happy for me dear ones.

You know I hold you dear, and be glad
I'm spending Christmas, with Jesus Christ this year.

I send you each a special gift, from my heavenly home above.
I send you each a memory of, my undying love.

After all "Love" is the gift, more precious than pure gold.
It was always most important in the stories Jesus told.

Please love and keep each other, as my Father said to do,
for I can't count the blessing or love he has for each of you.

So, have a Merry Christmas and wipe away that tear.
Remember, I'm spending Christmas, with Jesus Christ this year.

Author unknown

In loving memory of our precious

Preacher Tolbert Moore

Our precious Preacher Moore is home now with the Lord-
So many years he served and always preached the Word.
Our hearts are truly broken the tears are flowing free-
But the tears that we are shedding are just for you and me.

The man we loved so much is now settled with the Lord,
In no more pain, truly healed, according to God's word.
There is so much to say as we praise this precious man-
And yet the words escape us, we are trusting in God's plan.

Each sermon that he preached was sent from God above-
And delivered to his church with blessed Christian love.
As he yielded to the spirit each time he preached the word-
His prayers going to heaven for them to accept the Lord.

He freely shared his wisdom with younger preachers you see-
Giving such an advantage to folks like you and me.
Truly we will miss him but we have God's promise you see
That someday we'll be together again forever, for eternity.

Given to me by the Lord
Jerry Lee Schock

Coprighted 11/12/2021

In The Valley

My precious Father in heaven I make this petition today,
From the one I love so much please take his pain away.
Give him peace and comfort as You hold him close to You,
If only I could be there that's what I would do.
Let him feel Your presence in a valley that seems so deep
Give him peace and comfort and a very restful sleep.
The only thing in life on which we can depend,
Is the love You promised Your children and that will never end,
Today the clouds have gathered and he cannot see the sun
But brighten up his life Lord as each day is done.
In the valley he is walking You have already gone ahead,
You walked the path before him there is nothing he must dread.
Remind him that every valley has a mountain on each side
Looking ahead with You leading the valley is not so wide.
You promised in the valley you will restore our soul
And our cup will run over with mercy so we can again feel whole.

With love and prayers for Alex as you walk through this valley with the Lord beside you remember He has promised He will never leave us or forsake us. PSALM 23

Given to me by the Lord 10/11/21
Jerry :Lee Schock

Bearing the Burden

Gal 6:2 " *Bear ye one another's burdens, and so fulfill the law of Christ."*

Years ago as I searched for guidance to help a sister in need, God led me to this scripture. But Lord, how can I bear another's burdens? And the answer is intercession. The greatest intercessor is our Lord and Savior. *Rom. 8:34* "… It is Christ that died…who also maketh *intercession* for us".

<u>Could you? It is a Privilege-</u>

To think that the God of Heaven –so Holy and awesome-would allow the likes of any of us to come into His throne room, is truly humbling…but He does! And that is where we bear those burdens, through intercessory prayer. Intercession is defined as taking another's needs to someone in authority. What a privilege to be able to do something for someone else!

<u>Should you? It is a Responsibility-</u>

Galatians 6:2 says it is the law of Christ we fulfill. God looks for intercessors. Ezek 22:30 " And I sought for a man among them, that should make up the hedge, and stand in the gap before me …but I found none." Isaiah 59:16 "And he saw that *there was* no man, and wondered that *there was* no intercessor.." Many other scriptures exhort us to pray for one another.

<u>Would you? It is a Blessing</u>

Intercession changes YOU. It brings you closer to the Lord, and to those for whom you pray. We should listen very carefully when the Holy Spirit nudges us. Many times we are not listening as closely as we should and I often wonder what was lost. Is someone hurting –or in need of something that God would have helped –had I been more attentive to His voice?

Have you ever felt a tug to call someone or pray for them and not know why? What did you do with that thought ? Act on it or just let it go? If you "just let it go" you may have missed a blessing. A few days ago I was on my way to work and felt a strong urge to call a friend, just to say, "I love you and be careful". I followed the nudge God had given me, sharing it with her, only to hear: "It was just in time, you will never know how much I needed those words". No, but God knew.

It is an act of selflessness that takes time. We must pray, asking for God's will and continue to pray UNTIL we get an answer. That can be days or maybe even years. Eph 6:18 " Praying always with all prayer and supplication … perseverance…".

It will get your mind off you. Quickly you are before the throne and in the battle. Remember, it is a responsibility and at times the Lord wakes an intercessor in the middle of the night, to do battle for another. Many hours can be spent making intercession, and often as we pray and plead it can break our hearts. But then the blessing comes…the prayer may not be answered in the way we thought but God will always get the glory as we seek His will in the matter. 1 John 5:14 "And this is the confidence that we have in him, that, if we ask any thing according to his will, he heareth us"

My constant prayer is :Lord please help me be what I <u>should be</u> for You-so that I can be what I<u> need to be</u> for other's. There is no greater blessing than being used of God! May you see this truth as you intercede for others.

The Intercessor

Making sweet intercession-for all needs
great and small.
Trusting in God's wisdom-as on His
Name we call.
Lean not to thine own understanding –
trust only in the Lord-
And He will prepare all hearts,
according to His Word.
Standing in the gap we ask the Father
to meet your every need
To send wisdom and protection
from above
–as we pray and plead.

.Given to me by the Lord
Jerry L Schock

Jessica

It's hard to describe such a special one,
always ready to serve,
As her ship is sailing on the sea of life,
you will not see it swerve.
The rudder is held fast to keep
the pathway straight,
Through every stormy gale,
by the Holy Spirit, her mate.
Her pilot is the Lord as she
journeys on the way;
Holding fast to Jesus, each and
every day.

> For Miss Jessica
> as you sail through life,
> With love,
> Miss Jerry
> April 23, 2009

More Than A Pastor

You are more than a Pastor and much more than a friend
You pray for and look after the flock and love us without end.
You seek the will of God for all you have to do
And trust so much in the plans and things He has for you.
You've never failed to preach the Word –
and stay close to His own heart.
Vowing not to stray or from His will depart.
Only up in Heaven will the results of your service be known
So until we get to Heaven-I'll thank you on my own.
Thanks for all the prayers and all the sermons true-
For sharing many of the visions God has given you.
For giving of yourself and not asking for any return-
For showing God's love so freely as for lost souls you yearn.
Thank you my dear Pastor for everything you do
And let me say with love- Happy Father's Day to you.

Love and prayers
Miss Jerry
2006

As The Eagle Stirreth Her Nest

Written by Jerry L/ Schock

As the eagle stirreth her nest Lord Sometimes You must stir mine

There are things You will find in my life Lord That I should be leaving behind

Like the potter who's working the clay Lord You must remold my life anew

As the eagle stirreth her nest Lord Stir me up make me live for You

When I wander away from Your will Lord Stir me up do whatever You must do

When I forget what a price You've paid Lord Bring it back to mind anew

Let me ne'er forget what You've promised Let me always be close by Your side

As the eagle stirreth her nest Lord In Your love I want to abide

As the eagle stirreth her nest Lord Sometimes You must stir mine

There are things You will find in my life Lord That I should be leaving behind

Like the potter who's working the clay Lord You must remold my life anew

As the eagle stirreth her nest Lord Stir me up make me live for You

Through All Of My Trails

By Jerry Lee Schock

Through all of my trials, and they have been few;

One thing has been strongest His love has shown through.

There's no burden to heavy, no valley too wide

There's no problem I can't conquer, with Him my side

I've got Jesus, I've got love and more happiness than I ever dreamed of

And though my steps may falter and temptation is strong,

I just lean on my Savior and He rights the wrong

Through all of your trials though many they be

Just trust in the Savior and He'll set you free

He'll lighten your burden, help carry your load,

You'll find things so much better, along life's road.

Through all of my trials and they have been few

Trust Him as your Savior and He'll carry you through

All of your trails.

He's Always Near

By Jerry Lee Schock

Though the road seems long and dreary, Oft times you feel so alone
Though at times your heart seems weary,
 Remember the steps lead toward home.
Just remember that Jesus has promised,
He'll go with you each step of the way
Remember the sunshine will follow the clouds,
Remember the brightness of day.
At times it seems He's deserted you,
But remember, no one has ever cared more
When you're weary, hurting, alone,
The pathway you're walking toward Heaven
Is leading closer to home.
 When you've lost a loved one so dear to you,
And the hurt seems greater than you can bear;
Just remember that Jesus the Savior,
Has promised He'll always be near.
When you cross the sands of your trials, looking back the footprints you see
Remember He didn't desert you He carried you through to be free
When you walk the long road of trails, When you hurt, no ending you see;
Remember the Savior still loves you, And by your side He'll always be.

Jn 16:32 "Behold, the hour cometh, yea, is now come…
and yet I am not alone, because the Father is with me."
Heb. 13:5 "…for He hat said, I will never leave thee nor forsake thee

Written November, 1982 for Bro. Jim Schultz in the loss of his mother

Sent to self for copyrighting 3/29/1989

His Love For Me

By Jerry Lee Schock
12/1971

Chorus:

If your life has been empty and aimless as mine,
If you wander and you worry, you're wasting your time.
This is surely the answer, for you need the Lord,
He's a friend and a comrade who'll ne'er break His word.

I took Him for my Savior, one wonderful day,
I worked for a little while then put Him away,
The years passed so quickly, I forgot what I'd known,
But His will must be done, so He brought me back home.
Now serving my Savior, is what I must do,
The price that He paid, I must tell to you,
Many long hours He suffered, much pain and torment
And then they took my Savior, to a cross He was sent.
They drove nails in those precious healing hands,
And they cut Him and beat Him, into less than a man,
And not one word He uttered, to the last He held strong,
Asking only forgiveness, for all of the wrong.
So if you'll take the Savior, please serve Him today
Don't waste any time now, don't turn Him away,
He died for our sins salvation to give,
Take Him as your Savior, let Him your life live.

Chorus repeat.

I'm Not Alone

As I bow before Your throne, I know I'm not alone
But sometimes the fear will flood my mind,
And I need your touch another time
I come trusting in You only, know You'll never leave me lonely
As another trial I'm facing, As through this life I'm racing
My trust is only in You Lord, clinging close to Your Word
I need Your special touch Lord, for sometimes it seems too much
Though I fear what lies ahead, I know there is no need to dread
This trial I'm facing today, has passed by the throne of grace
I'll not be in this valley alone, my Father won't leave me on my own
And as I'm climbing the mountain I see,
The Hand of God and my Savior leading me
No I'll not climb this mountain alone,
For You've promised I won't be on my own
Although I know not what lies ahead,
Deep in my spirit I know there's no need to dread
I'm not walking on this road all alone
And I know the burden is not my own.
Although I know not what lies ahead,
In my spirit I know I have no need to drea

Written for Grady Calcote as he faced the unknown
September, 1999
By Jerry L. Schock

Given to me by the Lord

September, 1999
By Jerry L. Schock

I bow before an awesome God; I see His throne above,
I kneel before my Savior and His eyes are filled with love,
He's the reason I can sing today He set this captive free,
And I humbly bow to You my Lord who died on Calvary's tree.

Baby In A Manger

Given 'to me by the Lord 11-97
Jerry L. Schock
Play in Bb

Trio sings:

Oh Baby laying in a manger, this restless world could not have known;
That Baby laying in a manger, one day for sin would atone.

Solo:

This Baby grew into a young man, such a simple life He would lead,
But the young man as He was growing, knew one day for sin He would bleed.

Trio sings:

Oh Baby laying in a manger, this restless world could not have known;
That Baby laying in a manger, one day for sin would atone.

Solo:

The star that shown so bright in Bethlehem, told a story for you and me;
A story- that this dear Baby, would shine throughout eternity.

Trio sings:

Oh Baby laying in that manger, even then I think You knew,
Oh Baby laying in a manger, the sacrifice would surely be You.
Oh Baby laying in a manger, one day this restless world would see;
That Baby laying in a manger, would set the whole world free.

In loving memory of My Precious Sister Nita

By Jerey Lee Schock

For years we shared so many things traveling on life's way
With nothing but love between us each and every day.
For more than 51 years we shared a sister like love -
Even having the same birthday blessed from Heaven above.
We always talked about the Lord knowing all was in His hands -
If we would go to Glory or stay was a part of His perfect plans.
Every day as we talked; I still can hear that sweet voice say-
"You're my "bestus" and I love you -no
one can take your place"
Each thing that I would give her you'd think that it was gold-
Over time and time again how sweet it was I was told.
She loved her "Jerry" doll and would listen as it would sing
"That's what friends are for" as a smile it was sure to bring.
Her faith was real and sure as she'd pray and trust the Lord-
Depending on His love and promises in His precious Word.
Although for many years we would find ourselves far apart-
The love we felt for each other just deepened in our hearts.
I will miss my precious Sister until in Heaven we meet again
But have a peace deep inside knowing she rests with Him.

Ecc 3:1-2 To every thing there is a season, and a time
to every purpose under the heaven-
2 A time to be born, and a time to die 12/14/2019

One Heartbeat Away From Heaven

How far away is Heaven and when will I be able to go?
Only You have the answer Lord-it is not for us to know.
We never know when the time will come
for the Lord to call us home
And those we love are left behind, but never to be alone.

One Heartbeat Away From Heaven

How far away is Heaven and
when will I be able to go?
Only You have the answer Lord-it is not for us to know.
We never know when the time will come
for the Lord to call us home
And those we love are left behind,
but never are to be alone.

Safe and Secure in the Savior

As brother Dennis preached tonight God gave me these words
Lord willing it will be published in book number three

That I may know the Savior who died on Calvary
Who gave His life and shed Hid blood oh so willingly
The very heart of Himself is what He wants to give
Willingly I wait dear Lord so for You only I live
Meek and lowly I should follow my Savior every day
As I search the word of God He will lead me all the way
As I follow my precious Lord and feel the change within
I will behold the will of God as He takes on my sin
I know God's grace is sufficient to meet our every need
If only we will follow and let our Savior lead
One day we shall behold Him and His glory we will see
There will then be no more questions for all eternity.

Inspired by a sermon preached October 19, 2021
at Galilean Baptist Church by brother Dennis Petty.
Given to me by the Lord Jerry Lee Schock

The Answers

Sometimes we're in the valley, because we go astray,
We fail to follow Your will and walk the narrow way.
We cry out from that valley-for help from up above
And know You will answer-because of Your great love.

We look for help everywhere –You're the last one we seek,
And in the end we find ourselves –worn and very weak.
Father give us the wisdom, to avoid these great delays,
Help us seek Your will for us and always give You praise.

Let our finite minds see that all answers are with you,
And every promise in Your Word-will forever be true.
If we will seek the answers to all the questions in life-
From You and no one else-we will avoid so much strife.

You given every promise and the way that we're to live,
Left nothing in our lives to chance-truly the way to

The Father Cares

I do not know what trial you face or the road that you must take
But I know the Father in Heaven –cannot make a mistake.
No trials can come our way –or touch us in this place
Except it first is approved above-at the Throne of Grace.
So when the road is hard to walk and the pain you cannot bear-
Know the Father in Heaven –He cares and is always there.
He walked the road before you and knows each step ahead-
Just hold on my precious loved one-there is nothing you should dread.
Hold that precious promise in your heart that you'll never be alone-
And take the burdens to the Lord-lay them at the throne.

> Given to me by the Lord
> Jerry Lee Schock
> 02/15/21

The Gift

The gifts are such a big part- as Christmas we celebrate;
Children are so anxious-they can hardly even wait-
But the greatest gift we can receive is not found under a tree,
All wrapped in pretty paper with a card for you or me.
There is no price tag to remove or any receipt to keep-
It's not found on a shelf or in a window on the street.
You cannot buy it on the web or find it in the store.
It's not even on a wish list – nor sought much any more.
It's been rejected by many who did not understand-
God's gift of salvation, through Jesus-
is His greatest gift to man.

May this season find you blessed
Jerry L Schock
2006

The Gift

The gifts are such a big part-
as Christmas we celebrate;
Children are so anxious-
they can hardly even wait-
But the greatest gift we can receive
is not found under a tree,
All wrapped in pretty paper
with a card for you or me.
There is no price tag to remove
or any receipt to keep-
It's not found on a shelf or
in a window on the street.
You cannot buy it on the web
or find it in the store.
It's never been on a wish list –
and it's not sought much any more.
It's been rejected by many who
did not understand-
God's gift of salvation, through Jesus-
is His greatest gift to man.

May this season find you blessed
Jerry L Schock
From the Lord with love
2016

The Greatest Gift Ever Given

Some focus much on presents and what they will receive
We should focus on Your presence and pray they will believe.
Christmas is a special time as we celebrate Jesus' birth–
And ponder on the greatest Gift that ever came to earth.
You loved Your children so much –You sent Your only Son,
To light the way for sinners –so Heaven could be won.
The world is in such turmoil-but the solution is so clear,
Simply, share the greatest Gift with others-
As we thank our Father for Jesus this year.

Jerry L Schock
12/18/10

Celebrate the Saviour

The world is full of turmoil as it cries out for peace-
But the God of all creation-is in their minds the least.
Many search for things to buy and many overspend-
Finding nothing that will satisy their desire in the end.
What they really need is ***the*** gift sent from God above-
Given for our salvation-sent with lots of love.
There is no price to receive this gift, anyone can pay-
All one needs to do is invite Jesus in today.
He will come into your heart -change your life forever,
And promises a home in Heaven for us to live together.
So focus on the gift of God-to truly satisfy-
And ask Him into your heart-on Him-you ***can*** rely.

May He bless you and yours as we
Celebrate the Saviour
Given to me by the Lord
12/10/11
Jerry L Schock

Celebrate the Saviour

The world is full of turmoil as it cries out for peace-
But the God of all creation-is in their minds the least.
Many search for things to buy and many overspend-
Finding nothing that will satisy their desire in the end.
What they really need is ***the*** gift sent from God above-
Given for our salvation-sent with lots of love.
There is no price to receive this gift, anyone can pay-
All one needs to do is invite Jesus in today.
He will come into your heart -change your life forever,
And promises a home in Heaven for us to live together.
So focus on the gift of God-to truly satisfy-
And ask Him into your heart-on Him-you ***can*** rely.

May He bless you and yours as we
Celebrate the Saviour
Given to me by the Lord 12/10/11
Jerry L Schock

*We each wear
2 pink ribbons, and a
pin that holds them fast;
To honor Bertha and Lessie,
with a love that truly will last.
"God says you're gonna make it", and that is our message to you,
As you travel on this journey-
our prayers will see
you through.*

With Love,
Cindy Forrest and
The Galilean Choir

Gal. 6:2 "Bear ye one
another's burdens…"
Sept. 30, 2006

Happy Fathers Day

When God made the father- He had a special plan
He wanted one who would love and lend a helping hand.
Someone who would be a guide on the path of life-
Who would care for his children and also love his wife.
He planted deep within him a yearning for the Lord,
And gave him a desire to read God's Holy Word.
Today is set aside so we may give special honor-
To the gift God gave us that we call our father
Whether here with us or gone to Heaven above
Today we want to honor each of them with love.

From the Adult Auditorium
Sunday School Class
2006

Happy Fathers Day

You are more than a Pastor and much more than a friend
You pray for and look after the flock and love us without end.
You seek the will of God for all you have to do
And trust so much in the plans and things He has for you.
You've never failed to preach the Word –
and stay close to His own heart.
Vowing not to stray or from His will depart.
Only up in Heaven will the results of your service be known
So until we get to Heaven-I'll thank you on my own.
Thanks for all the prayers and all the sermons true-
For sharing many of the visions God has given you.
For giving of yourself and not asking for any return-
For showing God's love so freely as for lost souls you yearn.
Thank you my dear Pastor for everything you do
And let me say with love- Happy Father's Day to you.

Love and prayers
Miss Jerry
2006

With Loving Appreciation

How do we express the love we feel for you;
Or say how grateful we are for everything you do?
As we sing praises to the Lord, led by your own hand;
We know the sacrifices made-as in His will, you plan.
For all your dedication to the Galilean Choir-
For all the time we practice, each and every hour-
For all the love and memories that we have to share-
For letting each of us know just how much you care-
For never failing to be there for our every need-
For every prayer you pray and every loving deed.
Today we want to say thank you Cindy,
for all you've ever done,
And to speak our un-ending love,
From each and every one.

With Much Love and Appreciation,
Your Choir
August 2, 2008

88 GOD GIVEN *Poems* for ENCOURAGEMENT

And we know that all things work together for good to them that love God, to them who are the called according to his purpose.

—Romans 8:28

MISS JERRY LEE SCHOCK

Words of Comfort from the Heart

*To every thing there is a season,
and a time to every purpose under the heaven.*

—Ecclesiastes 3:1

MISS JERRY LEE SCHOCK

www.ingramcontent.com/pod-product-compliance
Lightning Source LLC
LaVergne TN
LVHW021735060526
838200LV00052B/3281